SUNDAY

Also by Thomas Lux

The Land Sighted (chapbook) 1970
Memory's Handgrenade 1972
The Glassblower's Breath 1976
Versions of Campana (chapbook) 1977
Madrigal on the Way Home (chapbook) 1977

The Houghton Mifflin New Poetry Series
Judith Leet, *Pleasure Seeker's Guide*
David St. John, *Hush*
Heather McHugh, *Dangers*
Gerald Stern, *Lucky Life*
Judith Wright, *The Double Tree: Selected Poems 1942–1976*
Christopher Bursk, *Standing Watch*
Thomas Lux, *Sunday*

SUNDAY

POEMS:

THOMAS LUX

HOUGHTON MIFFLIN COMPANY BOSTON 1979

Library of Congress Cataloging in Publication Data
Lux, Thomas, date
    Sunday.

    (The Houghton Mifflin new poetry series)
    I. Title.
PS3562.U87S8   811'.5'4   79–13251
ISBN 0–395–28349–3
ISBN 0–395–28350–7 pbk.

Printed in the United States of America
P 10 9 8 7 6 5 4 3 2 1

The poems in this book first appeared in the following magazines:
*Antaeus, Field, Footprint, The Iowa Review, The New Honolulu Review,
The Paris Review, Pequod, Ploughshares, Pocket Pal, Poetry, Quarry
West, Quarterly West, The Seneca Review, The Virginia Quarterly
Review.* The Dino Campana poems appeared first as part of a chapbook
titled *Versions of Campana* published by Pocket Pal Press, Jeanne Duval
Editions. The poem "View from a Porch" appears as a broadside
published by Sarah Lawrence College. "Barrett and Browning" appeared
in *Pushcart Prize, No. 2: Best of the Small Presses.*
    The author wishes to thank the National Endowment for the Arts,
which helped support him for a year, and the MacDowell Colony, where
some of these poems were written.

For Carol

For Jane Cooper, Grace Paley and Jean Valentine
and for my students at Sarah Lawrence College

"I ASK NOT OUT OF SORROW, BUT IN WONDER."
—Czeslaw Milosz

CONTENTS

I

SOLO NATIVE

Suppose you're a solo native here
on one planet rolling, the lily
of the pad and valley.

You're alone and you know
a few things: the stars are pinholes,
slits in the hangman's mask.
And the crabs walk sideways
as they were taught by the waves.

You're the one thing upright
on hind legs, an imaginer,
an interested transient.
Look—all the solunar tables
set with silver linen!

This is where you'll live, exactly
here in a hut on the green and gray belly
of the veldt. You'll be

a metaphor, a meatpacker,
a tree dropping or gaining
its credentials. You'll be

a dancer with two feet dancing
in the dirt-colored dirt. All this,
and after a few chiliads,

from your throat a noise,
an awkward first audible
called language.

THE GREEN

I don't know why the moth
on the other side of the window
beating the poor dust off his wings
I don't understand why
he wants to get in here. If

he did get in he'd have no visual
diversion but himself in the mirror —
which is all I have — and which is a boring
diversion. Meanwhile,

the clouds, between the earth
and the moonlight, are lame
and beg to be dispersed. I know the forest,
in the darkness, is still green

and I believe when it is nearly dawn
a sparrow will land on the chair
on my porch. The lower half
of her beak will be missing,
she can't eat,
and she is still alive.

RILKE AND LOU

"RAINER MUST GO."
—Lou Andreas-Salomé, from her journal

Of course, Lou noticed the angels
in Rilke's pockets and hat
but wondered: Does he have to be a poet
all of the time? That,
actually, wasn't the real problem.
Rainer was a sweetheart,
too sweet, hanging
around too much. Besides,
he practically wept every time
a leaf fell from a tree.
Jesus! thought Lou, this guy
will devour me, or try
at least — he's rather frail — so
let's unload him, fast.
Only because she had bigger genius,
you understand, than any poet,
any philosopher — Nietzsche's
a good example — and was certainly up there
in insights with Freud.
And, as we come to expect
from all illuminati,
she was angry
when she saw the other angels, angry
at the end
that they were coming.

THE BITTERNESS OF CHILDREN

Foreseeing typographical errors
on their gravestones, the children
from infancy — are bitter.
Little clairvoyants, blond, in terror.

Foreseeing the black and yellow
room behind the eyelids, the children
are bitter — from infancy.
The blue egg of thirst: say hello.

Foreseeing the lower lips of glaciers
sliding toward their own lips, the children
from infancy — are bitter.
Them, rats, snakes: the chased and chasers.

Foreseeing a dust-filled matchbox, the heart,
the temples' temples closing, the children
are bitter — from infancy.
From the marrow in the marrow: the start.

BARN FIRE

It starts, somehow, in the hot damp
and soon the lit bales
throb in the hayloft. The tails

of mice quake in the dust,
the bins of grain, the mangers stuffed
with clover, the barrels of oats
shivering individually in their pale

husks — animate and inanimate: they know
with the first whiff in the dark.
And we knew, or should have: that day
the calendar refused its nail

on the wall and the crab apples hurling
themselves to the ground . . . Only moments
and the flames like a blue fist curl

all around the black. There is some
small blaring from the calves and the cows'
nostrils flare only once
more, or twice, above the dead dry

metal troughs. . . . No more fat tongues worrying
the salt licks, no more heady smells
of deep green from silos rising now

like huge twin chimneys above all this.
With the lofts full there is no stopping
nor even getting close: it will rage

until dawn and beyond, — and the horses,
because they know they are safe there,
the horses run back into the barn.

DAWN WALK AND PRAYER

I step out onto the porch a few minutes
short of dawn

and hear the deaf
and nearly blind
old woman next door coughing.

Since this is the hour of exhaustion
and insomnia I'll walk for a while
on the beach since it's here

in front of me now as it usually
isn't. I love the light

at this hour — I call it dim
disappearing. I also love the boats:
flipped over, their hulls
turned to the sky. They're facts

of this world I would kiss
or at least caress: things that belong
underwater turned and touching

their opposite: air.
At this hour I could get away

with a kiss or a caress.
But I won't try — I'm thinking
about my neighbor. To be deaf

and practically blind
and now also with a cough:
That's why I'm making this prayer.

POSTCARD TO BAUDELAIRE

It's still the same, Charles.
Every day dislimned, the heart clicking
erratically — the sound of amateurs
playing billiards. How are you enjoying
the high privileges
of the dead? The double
triple and more turns
of the dark, the delicious
please of quietude? No one,
no thing is different: the oblati swarm,
the poor are formed into lines
leading poorer . . . There's one good thing,
Charles: the few beautiful verses
granted you by God
sing. Even though you're deaf
I want you to know
they sing! You should know that,
Charles, it's still the same.

ALL THE SLAVES

All the slaves within me
are tired or nearly dead.
They won't work for money,
not for a slice of bread.

Tired or nearly dead,
half underwater, wanting
merely a slice of bread:
the inner slaves, singing.

Half underwater, wanting
only a few flippers to swim,
the inner slaves, singing
the depth-charges within.

Only a few flippers to swim!
And a sensor to sense the sound
of the depth charges within —
that's all they ask for aloud.

A sensor to sense the sound,
a hearer to hear the small aurals:
that's all they ask for aloud.
They're slaves with slaves' morals.

Hearers hearing small aurals,
they won't work for money.
They're slaves with slaves' morals,
all these slaves within me.

GRAVEYARD BY THE SEA

I wonder if they sleep better here
so close to the elemental pentameter
of the sea which comes in incessantly?
Just a few square acres of sand
studded mainly with thick posts
as if the coffins beneath were boats
tied fast to prevent further drift.
I half stumble around one pre-dawn,
just a dog following the footprints
of another dog with me, and stop

before one particular grave: a cross
inlaid with large splinters of mirror.
Whoever lies here is distinguished,
certainly, but I wonder—why mirrors?
For signaling? Who? No, they're embedded
in the stone and so can't be flicked
to reflect the sun or moonlight.
Is the sleeper here unusually vain
and the glass set for those times of dark
ascensions — to smooth the death gown,

to apply a little lipstick to the white
worms of the lips? No again. I think
they're for me and the ones who come,
like me, at this hour, in this half-light.
The ones who come half-drunk, half-wild,
and wholly in fear — so we may gaze
into the ghosts of our own faces,
and be touched by this chill of all
chills, — and then go home, alive,
to sleep the sleep of the awake.

II

ELEGY FOR FRANK STANFORD
1949–1978

A message from a secretary tells me first
the heavy clock you were
in your mother's lap
has stopped. Later, I learn who
stopped it: you,
with three lead thuds,
determined insults, to your heart.
You dumb fucker, Frank.
I assume, that night, the seminarians
were mostly on their knees
and on their dinner plates only a few
wing bones — quiet flutes
ahead of the wind . . . I can almost
understand, Frank: your nerves'
oddometer needle waving
in *danger,* your whole
body, in fact, ping-raked, a rainbow
disassembling. You woke, in the dark,
dreaming a necklace of bloodsuckers. . . .
But that final gesture,
Frank: irreversible cliché!
The long doorman of the east continues
his daily job, bending slightly
at the waist to wave dawn past.
Then the sparrows begin
their standard tunes, every day, Frank,
every day. There's the good hammer-
music in the poles
of north and south; there's the important
rasp of snake over desert and rock;
there's agriculture — even when it fails:

needle-sized carrots, blue pumpkins;
and presidencies, like yours, Frank,
of dredging companies, but presidencies . . .
You must have been desiring exit badly.
So now, you're a bit of gold to pound
back into the earth, the dew, of course,
forever lapping your toes, —
Frank, you dumb fucker, — who loves you
loves you regardless.

SPIDERS WANTING

I want you, spider: walker-on-the-ceiling,
creeping black thumb.
Here's my forehead, the pad
or your landing. So slip
down your rope, that purest advance
of saliva, settle close
enough to my lips.

I'll know what you know,
thank you. Exhort, tell the story
of the eight-leggers. Put your fur
next to mine, relax down here
on the pillow. You look like a priest
in a multisleeved cassock
so let's confess

to each other: We're beasts,
twelve limbs between us,
sharing one house, the same desires
and industry: to design
the web, live on what we catch
from air, and always returning,
always, to the spun eluctable cave.

DIDACTIC

What is right is an obsession.
What is wrong is not.
Licking off birth-slime is right.
The strangle, one finger, fifth vertebra: wrong.
Swallowing a furry pill: also wrong.
Right: the sound of blood in a child's wrist.

What is right is an obsession.
What is wrong is not.

Wrong: giving the masters a bath
and putting them to sleep. Also stupid.
Those without tongues we teach
to speak. Impossible, therefore right.
What is right is an obsession.
What is wrong is not.

PORTRAIT OF THE MAN WHO DROWNED
WEARING HIS BEST SUIT AND SHOES

When his small skiff returned alone,
like a horse who's lost its rider,
the relatives sat down on stones

by the shore and waited for the tide
to bring him, also. He had wanted
to row back, singular and drunk,

from a wedding on a neighbor island,
just a few real miles away
across the black calm. The relatives

waited, the tide did
what it does, and he arrived
in that familiar pose

of all the drowned: face down, chin
tucked in, arms outstretched
with slightly cocked wrists,

and legs a bit splayed — the position
of a man trying to fly somewhere,
somehow. The Dead Man's Float

it's called by the living
which carried him home on a flight
both airless and lacking a wing. . . .

SOME TECHNICALITIES OF GRIEF

Some of the technicalities of grief
are: a ratty shroud, one sardine

for dinner, not living long enough
to wear out a favorite pair of shoes . . .
These are minor but true

technicalities — mere breath suspended
above something not so obvious
as a grave. When birds fly past

with lit matches in their beaks —
that's when to begin to worry.

If you build a sad dummy
of straw, your own shirt and pants,
and heave him off a cliff

only to have him die before he hits
bottom — then to be worried, more.

And the wind, the technical wind,
when it comes, crouched and invisible,
to carry you away down the black

chutes of the streets — then to be worried,
most, for a moment: the last ineffable.

MAN ASLEEP IN THE DESERT

He's the man — we all recognize
him — he's the man
in the desert who sees a mirage

of a frozen lake whose skaters glide
across its cold thirstless face.
On the warmer side of a dune

he reclines and pulls the palest sheet
up to his chin and sleeps, fitfully,
as only he deserves.

He dreams: Love as a tool,
love as a bribe.
He dreams: X, X, X, X, and he interprets these

as the particular zones of passion
he does not remember.
The moonlight, like a blue welt

of indignation, doesn't disturb him.
In his sleep he nods toward
the curved leaf of calm

and his pulse slows its vital imaginings. . . .
There is only one flaw in the window
of his sleep: Nothing on the other side.

THIS AIR

It's a whiteness that's pervasive,
or, *persuasive*, this air: a great sack
of blankness carried on the hump-backed
horizon. If it were blood

it would be so rare a donor
couldn't exist, or if he did, alone,
step forward. If it were water
it would be so gray and deep

you would not dip in your hand.
The one respite is sleep
and since sleep is not a man
or a woman or a child it can't

be grabbed by the heels
and dragged down a flight
of stairs, thus producing sleep.
No respite from this air — which is why

I love the moles who are blind
and who, wearing simple blue nightgowns,
come out only in darkness.
And which is why, in this air,

and on this ever-diminishing
page, no one, no one
will be saved, not even
the saviors.

THE ENEMY THE WIND

Hand over hand and over the backs
of some humans it comes

as it does now, from the south, south-
east. It comes, beginning nowhere

and hauling all the expelled
breaths of millions, from nowhere,

a foot or a thousand feet above
the oceans, carrying and not

caring. It comes — an enormous zero
that encircles whatever objects

it whirls around. It's this wind
that touches me here and maybe

again some endless miles north,
or west, or . . . In the back

of my eye it's always there
dividing whatever leaf from whatever

tree — dull, unrelenting, dumb.
And also its sour taste rattling

across my tongue. . . . O immortal
and awful marriage between velvet

between velvet pliers and a velvet
noose: the wind, the enemy.

LAMENT FOR THE FRIEND WHO LOST
HIS BROTHER

(—for Gary Wilson & IN MEMORIAM : Kenneth Wilson, 1943–1977)

The brutal shift: one minute
present — then a week on the delicate life raft

of coma — and the next: past.
You honestly begged for him
a few more diamonds of breath,
until the last luminant exhalation

exhaled. Your brother gone and the long o
sounds of your own children sleeping . . .
The grief is: one brother missing
and the other more alone.

— Hear the dogs? Hear your younger son's
small yelps just before waking?
And the snakes, hear them rustling
beneath the fronds

in their half-chilled sleep?
It's late. Soon you'll lean hard
on the bellropes, and dawn,

our daily cousin
will ascend. And you, you, — more alive
for what you've lost.

PAST TENSE

When I was barely human nobody loved me.
Ditto the other way around.

I was convinced the wrong arms
had been placed on my body

and at the same time convinced
only a coward tongues

the broken spine of his king.
My personality was as animated

as an empty shelf and even
my lapses were common. Therefore,

in the past tense, I bang my cup
against the bars of this cell

in disgust, of course, but mainly
because of the *sound* it makes.

III

GOLD ON MULE

On his knees with that pickaxe,
the sluice, the pan — all for a palm
full of dust. Valuable
eventually. Right now, the sun slams
on the wing of a fly
seeking moisture around the eye

of a mule waiting for his back
to be piled with gold. Poor bastard,
first he walks up here with sacks
of flour, beans, and sooner or later
leaves downhill, heavier, loaded.
It gets turned into money.

It's a sweat to get this stuff
and it's ugly from the rock.
The secret of minerals must be polish,
all the swipes of vanity applied
to what is really dirt. Rare
dirt, sure, but dirt on the spines

of mules — balanced like gold.
The man keeps digging, hacking out
a vein for what he needs: who
can name it? There's a slow shout,
nobody hears, in the air.
The man digs. The mule stares.

FARMERS

Force-feeding swans — let me tell
you — was hard. And up
every morning 4:30 counting

the lambs out to pasture,
each one tapped on the forehead with a stick
to be sure it's there.

Uncle Reaper half the time so drunk
he'd pull his milkstool
under the horse: more work

explaining the difference. Gramma
and Cousin Shroud putting up
8000 jars of beets, Auntie Bones

rapping her wooden spoon
against my ear: "More bushels, bumbler!"

I'll tell you — I understand
how come the dancing bear tore off his skirt
and headed back to the Yukon,
how come all of a sudden jewels in avalanche
down the spine of my sleep. . . .

But still, still when it rains
I remember all of us: farmers, simple sweat mongers
of the dirt whose turnips depend on it,

I remember how we called it down, how down
we desired it to fall: the rain.

POEM BEGINNING WITH A LINE
BY WALLACE STEVENS

It is all that you are, the final dwarf of you,
and regardless you go on — one foot

behind the other, wearing a small ladder
around your neck. It's a final

final dwarf that you are, a king
of dwarfs. You're proud
when the other dwarfs look down

at you. And prouder still
as you grow even smaller, —
like a birthmark on the neck

of one newly dead, like the red dot
on the horizon which has never
been so far away.

What you feel now
is so small it can't belong

to you. It belongs, instead,
to another feeler outside
of you, the smallest feeler

who sleeps between the enormous whorls
in your left palm, and who sings

only one tune: of the disappearing —
halved so many times, it does,
against all laws, disappear.

POEM BEGINNING WITH A RANDOM PHRASE FROM COLERIDGE

If there were anything
in the superiority of lord
to gentleman,

of gentleman to dog,
of dog to ort, of ort
to mote, of mote to . . .

Why always these assignations
of wrong names to wrong profiles?
Why's everything beside, divided?

Why one obsession, two obsession,
three, four, why always going back
and wanting more?

Somebody says: We're all in this together
and we board the lifeboats
in this order: first children, then poets,

then men and women fighting
it out — all our hearts stunned
and pinned like targets

over the hearts of all
men, women, every extant mammal,
moanworthies, all. . . .

MOST OF MY DISEMBARKMENTS

Most of my disembarkments
were possibly flawless,
graceful as the best music, graceful
as the pianist's ten fingers
who are all separate bodies
and lives. But even in my little finger
there was no kindness.

So, I decided to start again.
I started again and still
there was no kindness so
I decided to explore a single theme,
a theme I have never admired
except at the distance
from which I admire and admit

the number of breaths taken each day
in our considerable contests
of breathing. . . . Faithfully, night
and her chilled closet arrives,
and inside — this theme
in its nether language:
There are too many lost.

Here's the list:

POEM IN THANKS

Lord Whoever, thank you for this air
I'm about to in- and exhale, this hutch
in the woods, the wood for fire,
the light — both lamp and the natural stuff
off leaf-back, fern, and wing.
For the piano, the shovel
for ashes, the moth-gnawed
blankets, the stone-cold water
stone-cold: thank you.
Thank you, Lord, coming for
to carry me here — where I'll gnash
it out, Lord, where I'll calm
and work, Lord, thank you
for the goddamn birds singing!

BARRETT AND BROWNING

Mr. Browning helped but I think poetry
and hatred
for her father made Miss Barrett decide
to live. I think

I believe this dire couple.
And for once I believe
scholars: *they loved each other.*

Elizabeth, of course, was smarter.
Robert, in the beginning, more ardent.
He was positive

and if his main inventions
were in a field
other than verse
he would have invented the wheelchair

and pushed her
relentlessly south and warmer.
I'm sure this was one reason why
she got up and walked alone. . . .

Love helped, though, and they did
love each other — bearing
one healthy but dull child
and many healthy poems,
which, of course, is never enough. . . .

HERE'S TO SAMUEL GREENBERG

Here's to Samuel Greenberg
who died of bum lungs, age 23,
in 1916, penniless, leaving
only a few notebooks
as a gift to Hart Crane
who died of bum lungs (i.e., filled
with seawater), age 33, in 1932.
Here's to you, Samuel — semi-illiterate
coughing it out among total
illiterates during the only time
in your life you had time
to write: on your back,
on a cot, on Ward Island
preparing nearly inaudible gifts
of language, which were used,
as collaboration, in a few lines,
in a few poems by Hart
Crane — who had a little
more time to sing through his mouth.
Here's to you, Samuel Greenberg,
small master, and here's to your bones
which glow and are sliding
beneath the earth, with the earth. . . .

IV

from ORPHIC SONGS: Versions of poems by Dino Campana (1885–1932)

(*—for Bill Knott, who first introduced me to the poetry of Campana*)

JUST A POEM

I don't want peace. I can't endure war.
The world walks through me in a dream —
I'm silent, can't sing, I'm lonely,
Lonely but for my dear and ruinous songs.
— The mist filling an enormous harbor,
That's what I'd like.

Yes!, an enormous harbor
Crowded with velvet sails,
Ships undulating and anxious to lift
Anchor and head for the blue
Horizon, where only the lisp
Of the wind slips by in perfect hues.

And the wind carries these hues
Forever across oceans.
— I'm dreaming. Life is lousy

And I'm lonely, almost.
O how am I going to get out of here?
O when will my heart, stupid and trembling,
Wake up blind to the sun
The endless sun?

MISERABLE TIME

I hope this miserable time destroys me,
Me, my joy, my hope.
I hope the Pale One comes to me and says:
Let's go, Pal.
Lazy, lying in the grass,
Stuffed with food after lunch, even I,
Even me, Dino Campana, should have composed
Delightful poems
Dedicated to the insatiable
And nasty woman far enough away . . .
Always, since childhood,
A miserable kitchen gnawed at me
And ruined my exquisite taste . . .
Death, skinny and so serious,
Has a rhythmic voice
Which I still taste so completely.
But the world, which is fat,
Has kicked it out and mocks it.
Powerful are the rich these days.
They decide the laws
That say who goes hungry.
And for the poor who stumble
Across the earth?: an ideal, a starving
Ideal thrashing like a child
In a coma — trying to sell . . . what?
In brothels, for not touching
This ideal, the women
Raise their skirts. Some idiots have ruined
The holy moment that passes
And which will grant us tomorrow.
So immense!: the nervous, the lunatic

Break from the earth like mushrooms
After rain. And when they laugh
(As if they were on stage
And the only ones laughing at their own joke)
The toads and the tender
Frogs — who seem to be in rapture — accompany
Them in the moonlight
Like pearls hovering above dead flesh . . .
O Death, death, O old captain —
Even if you're diminished to a skeleton —
Hold out your arms to me
Like scythes and carry me, embrace me
Toward the stars.
O blind and hushed veteran
I hope between the hardness of your arms
My head will ring,
Frayed, electric, like a thread
That snaps.

THE BURNING TRAIN ON THE TAWNY PAMPAS

The burning train on the tawny pampas
Always ran and always won its race
And dizzily upset
The pure infinite infinitely.

She kissed me on the cheek
And this enormous and horrible continent
Switched its posture — quickly, endlessly.

So here's my book, and here it:

Here it comes limping —
My sonnet a salute to you.
Please accept it and its only virtue:
To sing distorted rhymes off-beat.
And when you meet the hour of death
I hope your soul returns to you
As you kneel to fondle the few
Odd things between your crippled legs.

· · · · · · · · · · · · · · ·

I'm looking for a word
One word for: spit
In your face, ram through you . . .
Merda! — right now I hope the Nobel Prize
Will be given back to the chemist
Who discovered that stinking word: dynamite.
Which I hope fouls the scarlet
Pig's blood in your veins,

Which I hope crushes your dorsal spine
So you'll die in the slime
And moss and vomit of your own pulp!

AUTUMNAL GARDENS
(Florence)

This is to the ghost on the lawn, to the quiet
Laurel wearing green wreaths,
To the dying earth — this is it:
A final goodbye!
On the barren red hillsides
In the dying sun,
Life on the horizon, its harsh cries
Merged, screams: screams
To the death-rattling sun that soaks
The flowerbeds with blood.
Like a knife a fanfare
Rises: the river disappears
Into the gold sand: the pale statues
Turned toward the bridge stand
In silence: already
Things are no longer.
And from beneath: silence,
Like a quietly impressive choir,
Rises and gasps up to my balcony:
And in the scent of laurel,
In the piercing scent of laurel
That lingers among the deathless
Statues in the sunset,
She appears to me, now.

THE GLASS WINDOW

From the highest window
The smoke of a summer evening
Pours light upon shadow
Burning a seal into my heart.
But who has (on the terrace on the river
Someone lights a lamp) who has,
Who is it, who has lit the lamp
At the little Madonna of the Bridge? —
In this room there's a smell
Of something putrid, in this room
A stale red wound.
The stars are buttons of pearls
And the evening wears a velvet shirt:
The inane evening trembles: the evening
Is inane and it trembles, —
But on the heart of the evening
There is, there is always
A stale wound, red.

CAMPANA, NAILED TO A BOULDER

O for christsake poetry kiss
The soul of things alive!
And close it in like the sun in May.
Forget the vanity of the poet's dreams
In the drugged mornings.
I hope your sound shines
On all the forms
That move, sing, scream —
Electric in the sun!
Vague soul of the earth,
Your many forms, drawn
Between sleep and life,
Now circle everything. . . .
And I, Campana, nailed to a boulder,
Stare at you O goddess
Even though you whip me,
Even though you melt me and toss me
Into the trembling ocean of yourself.
O poetry be a beacon,
Be for Campana a beacon, and for you
I will carry an offering
Beneath the unknown curves
Of the sea, your cathedral
Which is sometimes white, sometimes blue.
There a flaming circle will break free
From its white arc and fly
Toward the magical edges:
O Genoa, Genoa, Genoa!

SONG OF DARKNESS

The hues near dark grow slim:
Nervous spirits, I hope the dark is sweet
To the heart that's stopped
Loving! We must listen
To the beginnings of rivers,
Rivers, rivers that understand spirits,
Spirits that listen. . . .
Listen: the hues near dark grow thin
And to the nervous spirits
The dark is sweet:
Listen: Fate has beaten you:
For the lighthearted another life
Knocks at the door:
NO MORE, MORE, MORE.
Is there a tenderness to offset death?
Know who still hugs you,
Know the sweet woman who whispers:
NO MORE, MORE.
Here, the wind lifts and is gone:
Here it returns from the ocean
And here we listen to the breathless heart
That loved us more!
Let's look: the trees and water
Are already like night,
The river moves in its speechless way. . . .
Bang!, Mother, the man up there!

V

TEACHER TALKING TOO MUCH
(—for Kathy Wallach)

A student complains: "That biology
teacher wants us to follow one kernel of corn
all the way from the sow pig's mouth
all around intestines right
to the left foreleg of one of her babies
in her belly, I mean can you
what's the point
of that?" The poetry teacher
says: "Sounds like an interesting journey."
And sets his thoughts out
subtly — as if balancing
a rowboat loaded with bricks
on a wave tip, as if retrieving
a hatchet wound
to the forehead: "I've been meaning
to talk to you about something,
a thing similar, cyclical, I suppose.
Consider that I'm talking
to myself as well as you.
Then consider the man or the woman
chained to the oar
next to yours. He or she — the immediate
thread here is cycle or voyage — rows
twelve-, sixteen-hour shifts
to the drumsound. Why?
For food, a little, air,
and the whip. And why do we
row, or imagine the rowing?
Because each of our cells is a singer
in the choir beyond the universe!"
Pauses. Not so hot. But continues:

"What's wrong with loving the voyage
of a kernel of corn? One lonely
nodule, yellow, like a chip of edible gold,
cruising the beautiful belly
with all its turns and slues: food for food
for what will be food.
Look close! — our eyes devices
of metaphor: see, imagine!"
No stopping him now: "Sure
pollution's a problem
but worse about the air is its crackling
with idiocy; and the swatch
of sky — is it the same
swatch always? — always there
with its motto: *What is inane endures.*
If we allow it. Look, I insist
that you infiltrate your life!
Go it agape, beliefs ambidextrous,
stumped with wonder, but enter it — so
as not to come to the middle, or before,
talking to your soup. Enter it
without leaving veins unlit,
without shattering alms boxes.
Enter it not as flamingoes enter mud flats
during drought — those lovely
paralytics — splayed, famished . . .
It's really a slingshot we lie in
thinking: hammock.
— Which brings us back, naturally, to the sky,
the air where we notice
the various chips of blue

drifting down and are pleased
the angels are sculpting, changing
careers in mid-career.
The sky is a chant and, unless
it is a war chant, it lulls.
If we count the needles
on the pine forest's floor
let's do it at night, with one hand
blocking the moon, and know
each one by touch. Let's not ride
the same donkey until our knees scrape ground,
not take exit signs as commands.
Let's unlash ourselves from the metronome!"
He's still talking — one person
talking to another who started it all
with hope. It's the listener who provides
and provokes the metaphor for the talker
and, in the same way animals love turning over
fallen apples with their noses in orchards
near dawn — they love each other. . . .
But it's science that initiated
this. He shifts to understatement
for emphasis: "Not much happened
in the pond today, just a few zillion
births, the algae
going berserk perfectly in tune
with the swimmers' indolent backstrokes. . . .
But there are some things
I want to talk to you
about: metaphor, how to shed, maybe,
the lachrymals, the rare lenses

permitted imagination. . . .
And there are some things
I'd like to sing with you
about: hog, corn, the poem, belly,
the nouns bearing blood types; and sky,
the sky full of shipwreck and joy,
the sky full of fires — to extinguish or feed."

CAPABLE AS HIVE

(—for Carol)

We begin every night ignorant,
two xenophobes called in from exile,
pleased nearly to the point of buoyant.
Fevergiving we'll name our glad child.

By dawn, a change is perceptible.
Both of us — our faces and four ears smeared
with honey, mouths open, capable
as hive — one, two, duo mutineers

ready to walk the circular planks.
Against the air is the way we lean.
— For the love we do there's not much thanks,
for the love we do succeeds each dream.

VIEW FROM A PORCH

Thud, thud, all the sores go blind,
and over the basket of pears hover
brief addicted fruitflies.

The bruises on the pears are also blind.
The barn is blue — as far
from the Mediterranean as possible.

You'd think the residents serious here — each one
scattered lonely as a cow-pie — you'd think:
blood-in-the-rafters. . . . But if you listen,

both ears, close, you'll hear a plow parting
earth; closer, some worms unburied
nervous. The chirpers are happy,

the humans go about jobs — in barn,
field, or house — healing,
unhealing, and sky again

is admitted to the dumb-lovely dirt
turned over and over, turning
its worn yawn wide: breathing, nearly alert.

MAN ASLEEP IN A CHILD'S BED
(—for Crystal Reiss, who loaned me hers)

Here's a man who falls hard asleep,
who sinks beneath the rim of air humming
a dim song, a threnody.
With him is a drowsy animal, his tongue,
and also the inner curtains of the mirror.
Only one thing visible: a small *oh* of breath.

Above the sleeper: one circle called breath.
A wedding ring of oxygen above a mouth asleep
and the long backward glance of the mirror.
There's a particular tune to his humming,
the tone is familiar, the tongue
comfortable, and the threnody

nearly light, a light threnody
of the lungs being lungs, the breath
riding back and forth over the tongue.
Here's a man fallen hard asleep.
Now here's the sleep-chortle, the humming
man behind the two-way mirror

of a dream, of a dream of a mirror
black on both sides. His threnody
is deep now, not quieter, his humming
deeper. He takes a breath, another breath,
innumerables. . . . He's far asleep,
and asleep in his mouth: his tongue.

Resting, it's an ancient tongue,
the one every man presses to the mirror,
every woman presses, while asleep,

to the glass, the faint threnody
which is a repetition of certain breath.
This is a surviving sleeper, humming

a constant tune, a raw humming,
quiet down to the root of the tongue.
Quiet like the gone breath
of the dead who moved and left a mirror,
who left, who left a threnody.
He is asleep and with them, asleep.

He's humming now, deep, the mirror
draws in its tongue, the threnody
is breath, and the dreamer's body, asleep.

THE HUNTING

Killing anything was pure accident.
A dumb stalker, a worse shot — I went
almost daily, to the woods.
A favorite prey was slow

and shallow: a brook.
I'd say, as it moved languidly:
Don't move, you rascal! And when it did,
of course, as it does, I'd shoot.
I liked that: no wound,

or at least a wound that healed
instantly. Once, however, a rogue
squirrel came into my scope
and stayed there, like a nut, eating

nuts, for half an hour.
Meaning only to frighten, I aimed about
a foot above and to the left: one shot, dead

between the ears. Thereafter, to guarantee
life, I aimed to kill, and thereafter
never did. I did love and dread

those scraggly woods, particularly
the getting to the center,
where, in snow or summer, I'd sit,
rifle across my knees, waiting

there at the heart of it
for something — silent, armed: a failure
and pleased with my failing.

FLYING NOISES

* * *

The horses out of their brains bored all
winter gnawing on stalls
Outside the snow several fetlocks deep
Pounding our noses
against the ice everywhere
you could say
we had our souls in backward
we were dumb from trudging away from noon
we were lame like the bread that lies on the table
One child's dream sledding down a slag heap
every day going at it with the cold

* * *

So he deposits the moth in a matchbox
and flails with a flashlight
into the forest a mile or two fox-
like crosses a few gullies streams
stopping finally beyond a final ravine
where he slides open removes the moth
lays down the light on the perfect
theater of moss
as backdrop a few slim branches
and on that greenly illuminated stage it dances
to an audience of darkness plus one

* * *

He was absolved prematurely they forgot
what he might do from the point
of absolution to the next point what's it called
So he filled in he could do anything
He disregarded the live hearts
of live humans he did misconduct before
his mother and father he coveted
his neighbor's wife and speedboat
he propped open a baby's eyes with matches
He did it like a good thief
having already been absolved

* * *

The mattress always acts as a raft
He's aware of that that's why he hopes
to bob in the wakes there
He never takes a path nonchalantly solo
knowing that's of course where
beasts do their dreaming also
He joins nothing He joins the other peasants
waving pitchforks not getting
dung for our wheat we've had it
up to our haircuts thinking we're salved
until we're mistaken is obvious

* * *

Approximately dawn some people exercise Take X
He goes out to a dirt road
with a club and bashes small stones
like in a ballgame Sending
a shot deep into the east slows down dawn
The first peeps of light In India
they have a word for it it's a child's name
you can't make a close paraphrase
The very beginning light
when roof and bush and animal
become apart from air

* * *

As if hands undoing our clothes from the inside
we fumble around in a rowboat
One oar floats downriver What a day
On the opposite shore Mallarmé's
feeding some swans How will we row
Which port our oars arriving
days ahead of us With you
voyaging you also voyaging
There's the lovely sword of moon
There's the cricket warming up his cello
There's the various positions in which we exult

* * *

Once gone like gloss in a flashflood
Once an animal loving another of another species
Once one joyful crumb of the fully individual
Once a convict dreaming of mowing a hayfield
Once an avenue upon a bench sits one moment of present
Once under deep enough to ring the literal sleep-bells
Once the dead changing shirts in their small booths
Once farmers merely bored by drought
Once all the birds invented as toys
Once the heart-angles the trillion u-turns of blood
Once the flying noise

* * *

Slow tarantula slow blink by blink
the afternoon unspools a wind primping
the fir tree's common hair
A blue calf bleats in the far pasture
Reduced by bucolia
it always hauls him back
gaping like a lump of gold shocked
in the sludge-sifter's hand
One water moccasin rolls over a few times
A hill hunches somewhat
while memorizing the earth's sore fictions

* * *

His mouth connecting lines the puzzle
from nape to the slope beneath
her ankles the dunes He takes
pleasure there and giving it it's simply the hearts
simply the lungs simply two
to swerve beneath the fell cleavers of day to day
Their nerves on overdrive together
two odd ones warbling around an oasis
alert to the blue thuds in the wrist
And that other pulse the pulse of top lip
to bottom lip and bottom lip to top

* * *

Loving the incunabula the beginnings
like one obsessed by desert
loving its freeze at night
because it reminds him more of water
than the heat of afternoon Lined
up and loaded like something on wheels
small wafers of anger off his bureau
spinning A window is open
On the table there is sky
And behind the curtain one marvelous belly
or else the wind is bringing the usual